fairyland books

COZY GARDENS

COMFY AND CUTE COLORING BOOK

This book belongs to :

_____

TEST COLOR PAGE

CUTE PATTERNS

STRAWBERRY

FLOWER

HEART

MUSHROOM

A BLANK SHEET OF PAPER

COZY COLORING COMMUNITY

Come hang out in our cheerful coloring hub
where creativity and kindness go hand in hand!

SHARE YOUR ARTWORKS

Bring your one-of-a-kind style to life.
We can't wait to see your masterpieces!

www.fairylandbooks.com

THE RAINBOW
AFTER THE RAIN

CRYSTAL OF POWER

THE FLOWER
OF CALM

Pinch of Magic

Soothing
Magic Brew

DREAM CATCHER
OF PEACE

THE FLAME OF
HOPE

POTION OF
JOY AND
POSITIVITY

Little
surprise

Hope you enjoy the coloring page!

fairyland books